How to Self-Publish Your Own Quilt Catalog:
A Workbook for Quilters, Guilds, Galleries and Textile Artists

By Kyra E. Hicks

Black Threads Press
Arlington, Virginia

ISBN: 978-0-9824796-0-5

Library of Congress subject headings:
1. Authorship
2. Self-Publishing – United States
3. Art – Marketing

Cover photo credit: NLshop on Bigstock.com
This book was created on a PC using Microsoft Word 2010. The interior font is Georgia. Version 1.0.

Contents

Yes, You Can Publish Your Own Catalog!

Will any of my quilts survive to be seen and enjoyed in 100 years or more? Who will know I quilted? Who will study my stitches and understand what I was trying to achieve with a bit of cotton and Coats & Clark threads. I think about these things.

I love historical research—following leads from microfilmed newspaper articles, dusty, out-of-print books, and interviews with someone who knew someone. I love "finding" on eBay or Amazon out-of-print gallery catalogs that introduce me to artists I hadn't heard of before.

Since 2003, I've had five books published on some aspect of quilt history. The first book, *Black Threads: An African American Quilting Sourcebook* was traditionally published. I self-published the books that followed—and had a ball! The technology for book publishing has evolved to be accessible and affordable.

Today many quilters and textile artists post photographs of their work on their Facebook profile, Flickr account or guild website. Will the digital images on these websites survive a decade or more?

I'm being selfish. The historian in me wants to learn about the works of other quilters and textile artists. I want to learn about artistic motivations, new techniques and styles. I want to read a book about the quilts stitched by a law professor in Alabama and understand how his quilts differ from a quilter in Omaha, Nebraska or a home-schooling mother in Georgia or the career women quilters in New York or Los Angeles. I want to learn about quilters in England, Canada, Japan, Liberia and other places. If such quilters create their own art catalog, then you and I just might be able to read such books.

In my blog, www.PublishYourQuilts.blogspot.com, I host a series of posts to share how you can create your own 24-page, full-color catalog.

If you know how to use Microsoft Word, have Internet access, and at least a dozen or so photographs of your art pieces, then you have the tools to *publish your own catalog*. Really—a full-color book about your artwork—and have it available for sale on major online bookstores.

This workbook is published using Microsoft Word and the same print-on-demand (POD) technique suggested for your own catalog.

I'll share here and on the blog some of what I've learn from self-publishing quilt-related books. I am not, however, available to consult with you individually.

I hope you are inspired to ***publish your quilts***!

Kyra E. Hicks
Arlington, VA

Step 1: Create a Theme for Your Quilt Catalog

Think about the different catalogs you've seen in art galleries. Usually, they are 24 or 36 pages and have an essay about the artist or theme of the exhibit. Then, there are several full-page photos of the artwork on display with captions about the work. There might also be an artist resume.

You can easily do this! You can create a catalog of just your work, or you can join your best friend and create a book with both your quilts. A guild might use this series of steps to create a full-color exhibit catalog for a local show.

The goal is to help you create a 24-page, full-color catalog available for sale on Amazon, the largest online bookstore worldwide.

What kind of quilt catalog would you like to create?

- A formal catalog showing your quilts – professionally photographed
- A casual catalog of your quilts covering beds or draped over the living room sofa
- A catalog dedicated to a series of quilts you've made...maybe your family-themed quilts, floral quilts or specific story quilts
- A statement of you as an artist or quilter with a mix of photographs of your artwork and you in your studio creating new works
- A catalog that features your quilts and poetry
- A catalog that includes your quilts and a quilt pattern you've designed
- A catalog that focuses on your creative process and how you make a quilt. The photographs could include your inspirations for the quilt, your various sketches to make the quilt, and the finished piece.
- A catalog featuring your quilts and other needle arts, such as doll making, knitting, crocheting, clothes sewing or needlepoint
- A catalog featuring quilts made by different generations in your family
- A catalog highlighting research you've done on one or two selected quilts

---

Assignments:

1. Take time to consider what is motivating you to publish your own catalog and who your potential audience for the catalog will be.
2. Write down potential themes for your own quilt catalog.
3. Select a theme for your catalog.

Step 2: Become Familiar with Print-on-Demand (POD)

Let's face it; a traditional publishing company is not likely to publish our quilts unless we're a well-known quilter or textile artist. But, documenting our quilts and our lives as quilters is important.

Publishing technology, the Internet and online buying have come together in such a way that you can affordably create a book and offer it, if you'd like, online for folks around the world to purchase. The technique called "print-on-demand" allows for as few as one copy of a book to be printed once it is purchased online. There are several companies that other quilters have used to publish work using print-on-demand such as CreateSpace, Lulu, and Blurb, to name a few.

Blurb.com – great for photo books, but is expensive because of the *fabulous* paper quality. Potentially limited sales as one can only purchase from the Blurb website.
- Allows you to create your book interior using Blurb software and templates
- Offers full-color softcover and hardcover books in seven different trim or book sizes
- Allows you to set the retail price of your book over the minimum book cost
- Offers optional Preview feature to sample the book prior to purchase

Lulu.com – founded in 2002, easy to publish for novices.
- Offers Microsoft Word templates by book size – you can just start typing
- Offers both soft covers and hardcover books (with and without dust jackets)
- Offers full-color interiors with as few as 32 pages in seven different trim sizes
- Offers two different paper grades for color: Lulu Standard and Premium
- Allows book covers to be designed using a free online "wizard"
- Offers distribution on Amazon.com and other book outlets

CreateSpace.com – owned by Amazon, easy to publish for novices.
- Offers Microsoft Word templates by book size
- Only paperbacks books are available
- Offers fifteen full-color book sizes, each allows for as few as 24 pages
- Just one paper option for color books - white paper
- Offers a free Cover Generator for you to build your own book cover
- Offers distribution on Amazon.com and other book outlets
- Books printed using CreateSpace can ship within 24 hours of ordering and be eligible for Amazon's Search Inside!™, Amazon Prime™, and Super Saver Shipping™ programs.

Assignments:
1. Visit each site, research its offerings, and read its Terms and Conditions.
2. Search for quilt and textile books published on these sites.
3. Determine which site offers features that are most important to your catalog creation, personal and sales goals.

Step 3: Learn How POD & Traditional Publishing Differ

The process for publishing any book involves many steps and considerations. Let's review the major elements to consider when selecting a print-on-demand vendor. You'll have to decide which elements are most important to you and how to approach each.

Below is a table that compares traditional publishing to print-on-demand so that you can see the various steps you'll go through with your own catalog. Don't be discouraged; every book has to go through this process. Your quilt catalog will too!

	Traditional Publishing	Print-on-Demand (POD)	Your Notes
Manuscript Ownership	Retains ownership of your manuscript	May or may not retain given terms and conditions	
ISBN	Publisher's ISBN	POD vendor or you buy your own	
Secure Permissions	You are responsible for securing and, if needed, paying for usage right (e.g., photos, models)	You are responsible for securing and, if needed, paying for usage rights	
Book Title	Publisher decides	You decide	
Editing	Publisher does	You do or pay someone else to do	
Book Layout	Publisher does	You do or pay someone else to do	
Book Cover Design	Publisher does	You do or pay someone else to do	
Printing	Publisher does, usually in large run sizes	Printed upon sale of as few as one single copy	
Distribution	Publisher does	Critical to select vendor that makes your title available to major online vendors, with large number of potential buyers (e.g., Amazon or BN.com)	
Marketing	Publisher does - given sales potential	You do or pay someone else to do	

Step 4: Consider the Components of a Book

When you were a kid, did you ever get some blank paper, fold it and staple the paper in the center fold to make a "book"? At its most basic, a book is a collection of folded pieces of pages.

The content of your book or catalog is critical to its success. The physical structure and layout of the book is also important in guiding the reader through the material. Here is a list of common book components from which we'll create a simple catalog layout.

Book Component Considerations for Your Quilt Catalog

1. Measurement – 7 x 10 inches, 8.5 x 8.5 inches or other trim size
2. Feel – hardback (with or without a dust jacket) or paperback
3. Paper – white or cream color, weight and brightness
4. Pages – number of pages

Front Matter	Body	End Matter
Title page	Introduction	Appendix
Frontispiece – decorative illustration facing title page	Body chapters – major sections	Bibliography, "Recommended Reading" or "Helpful Websites" lists
Title, subtitle, author's name	Chapter headings Subheadings	Notes page
Copyright page	Bylines	Endnotes
Dedication page	Header	Glossary
Epigraph – quotation	Footer	Index
Table of contents	Page numbers	About the author(s)
Lists – figures, illustrations or tables	Fleurons – decorative elements for separation	Teasers, excerpts or list of other books by the author
Foreword	Notices – tips or text set apart	Reader-response form
Preface	Photos or Illustrations	Advertising or order form
Acknowledgments	Footnotes	Colophon – details about how the book was made
Errata – list of corrections	Epilogue	

Assignments:

1. Flip through two favorite books. List 3 – 5 book components or formatting styles you had not noticed previously.
2. Determine the trim or book size for your catalog.

Step 5:   Determine the Interior Layout for Your Catalog

Today you get to create the framework for your own quilt or art catalog! Below are examples of a 24-page and 36-page catalog layout. You'll note various book layout conventions such as title page on the right-hand side of a book, while the copyright page is traditionally on the left. This exercise will also help you to gather the necessary elements, such as number of photos, for your catalog. See, when you sketch the layout for your catalog, it's not that intimidating!

Your catalog will be full-color. Color printing is more expensive than black and white. As a result, you have to be mindful of page count. The more pages in your catalog, the higher the book cost.

Quilt Catalog Layout

Page Number	24-Page Catalog	36-Page Catalog	Layout Your Catalog Pages
1	Title page (right side)	Title page (right side)	
2	Copyright page (left side)	Copyright page (left side)	
3	Dedication page (right)	Dedication page (right)	
4 – 5	Blank page – Essay text	Blank page – Essay text	
6 – 7	Text – text	Text – text	
8 – 9	Text – text	Text – text	
10 – 11	Text – photo	Text – text	
12 – 13	Photo – photo	Text – photo	
14 – 15	Photo – photo	Text – photo	
16 – 17	Photo – photo	Text – photo	
18 – 19	Photo – photo	Text – photo	
20 – 21	Photo – photo	Text – photo	
22 – 23	Photo – photo	Text – photo	
24 – 25	Artist Resume on page 24 – no page 25	Text – photo	
26 – 27		Text – photo	
28 – 29		Text – photo	
30 – 31		Text – photo	
32 – 33		Text – photo	
34 – 35		Text – photo	
36		Artist Resume – no page 37	

Step 6: Let Your Title and Subtitle Market Your Book

How do you go about buying a book? No, really. Take a moment to think about the different ways you buy a book from a traditional bookstore vs. an online bookstore or even your mobile phone or eReader, such as a Kindle or a Nook device.

There is little chance that your quilt or art catalog will be stocked by a traditional bookstore. As a result, you need to create a catalog title and subtitle that will have to work hard to attract potential buyers 24/7 who are online or using a mobile phone. These buyers are likely using a search engine, such as Google or AOL Search, or using the search box on a popular online bookstore to locate books. The keywords you include in your book title and subtitle to describe or position your catalog become very important.

For someone looking for a book about a specific quilter, they will likely type in the quilter's name and descriptive keywords such as: quilt, quilter, quilts, patchwork, appliqué, or type of quilt the quilter usually makes. They may also type in something distinctive about the quilter, such as geographic location, religion, or ethnicity.

Consider the keywords you might have used to locate these books:
- *Nancy Crow: Quilts and Influence*
- *Velda Newman: A Painter's Approach to Quilt Design*
- *Paula Nadelstern's Kaleidoscope Quilts: An Artist's Journey Continues*
- *Dancing at the Louvre: Faith Ringgold's French Collection and Other Story Quilts*
- *Erika Carter: Personal Imagery in Art Quilts*
- *My Quilts and Me: The Diary of an American Quilter by Nora Ezell*
- *Martha Mitchell of Possum Walk Road: Texas Quiltmaker*
- *Martha Skelton: Master Quilter of Mississippi*
- *Rosey Grier's Needlepoint for Men*

What keywords would someone use to discover your catalog? What theme are you trying to communicate in your book? Visit www.google.com/insights/search/ to see how popular your keywords have been worldwide or by country since 2004.

Assignments:

1. List potential keywords to describe your catalog.

2. Play with potential titles and subtitles for your catalog.

3. Visit Amazon and type in your potential catalog title. What competitive books are returned in the search results?

Step 7: Format Your Microsoft Word File

In Step 4, you should have decided on your catalog's trim or book size. Now you'll need to format the file you'll use to type your manuscript into this book size.

I use Microsoft Word when creating a book manuscript. Yes, there are software programs, such as InDesign, for properly formatting book interiors. However, for those who don't have access, can't afford, or don't want to learn a new program such as InDesign, Microsoft Word is an adequate program for your quilt or art catalog.

The print-on-demand company you use to print your catalog will likely have a Word or other template you can start typing into. For this series of blog posts, I suggest using CreateSpace to create your quilt catalog. You can find the CreateSpace templates by going to the website, clicking on Community text link > Resources > Formatting Your Files > Documents.

You can visit PublishYourQuilts.blogspot.com to download free Word templates in sizes 7 x 10 inches or 8.5 x 8.5 inches.

If you don't use a template, you'll need to set your own file settings. You can make note of your file settings in the table below.

	Option 1	Option 2	Your Catalog Notes
Paper Size	7 x 10 inches	8.5 x 8.5 inches	
Font	Georgia	Georgia	
Font Size	12	12	
Margins			
Top	1"	1"	
Bottom	1"	1"	
Inside	0.75"	0.75"	
Outside	0.75"	0.75"	
Gutter	0.25"	0.25"	
Multiple Pages	mirror margins	mirror margins	
Orientation	Portrait	Portrait	
Layout			
Header			
Footer			
Justification	Left and Right	Left and Right	

Step 8: Type Your Catalog Just as It Would Be Printed

One secret to creating your own quilt catalog using print-on-demand is that *you'll need to type and format your manuscript just as each page would appear printed.*

By now you should have determined the trim or book size for your catalog. The notes you took in Step 5 to determine the interior layout of your catalog will be your roadmap.

Open the Word file you formatted in Step 7 and start typing your ...
- Title Page. Center your title and sub-title as you would like to see it printed. Press Enter several times until you are onto the next page.
- Copyright Page. Be sure to copyright your work by typing Copyright © Year Your Name.
- Dedication Page.
- Blank Page. If you have a dedication page in your catalog, you might need a blank page following the dedication page. The text of a book typically starts on the right-hand side of the book. This blank page will force the text to start on the right-hand side. I usually type "This page left blank on purpose" to remind me to delete that sentence before I finish the manuscript completely.

As your manuscript becomes more complete, you might consider saving the file under a different version number, such as CreateMyOwnCatalog_v1 or CreateMyOwnCatalog_v2 and so on.

Your Manuscript File Name

You don't want to lose your manuscript so consider also setting Microsoft Word to automatically create a backup file and/or automatically save your file every ten minutes.

You may not feel as if you can use Microsoft Word well enough to format your catalog for publication. If you can afford it, the print-on-demand company is likely to have a service where you can pay a professional to format your catalog. You might also explore websites, such as Elance.com, for a freelancer to format your catalog.

Step 9: Write Your Catalog Essay

The next step in this project to create your own quilt catalog is to write the essay for your catalog.

For an artist catalog, you might consider writing an autobiographical essay to help readers understand how your life has influenced your quilt making. Your essay may be in prose format or in a question and answer format. Here are a few starter questions you might consider answering for an autobiographic essay:

- Early Life – What year were you born? Who are your parents, siblings?
- Education – Where have you studied? Did you formally study textiles?
- What year did you learn to quilt? Who or what influenced your decision to quilt? Did anyone in your family quilt?
- How does quilting make you feel?
- What do you hope to accomplish with your quilt making?
- How would you describe your quilt making style?
- How has your quilt making evolved over time?
- How many quilts have you stitched in your career? How long does each take?
- Where do you do your quilt making? Do you have a special room or studio? How does this space influence your quilt making?
- How does your family and friends support your artwork?
- How, if at all, does your culture or religious beliefs influence your art?
- What influence does your community or guild membership(s) have on your quilt making?
- How important are tools, such as fabric, sewing machines, and/or workshops, to your quilt making?
- What other needle arts do you do?
- How would you like the world to remember you as a quilter?

If your catalog is about an exhibit or series of quilts, you might consider answering:
- What inspired the series or exhibit?
- How does the series fit into the body of your art work?

Once you have written your essay, it is critical to have it proofed. Readers are not just buying images of your artwork, but also your words. Ask friends you trust for feedback on your essay. Have someone, with fresh eyes, review your essay for proper grammar and formatting.

Assignment:

1. Type your finished essay into your Word file.

Step 10:   Insert Your Photos and Write Your Captions

No art catalog is complete without photographs! I have several exhibit catalogs published in the 1970s, 1980s, and 1990s that have B&W photographs because this was the affordable way to publish such gallery catalogs. With print-on-demand, you can publish a catalog in full-color.

By now you should have determined the layout you want for your quilt catalog as well as the number of images or photographs you want to include.

There are a variety of photographic styles you can use for your catalog, such as:
- Professionally or personally photographed art pieces;
- Images of you at work sewing on your machine or sewing by hand;
- A photograph of your quilt on a bed or wall; and/or
- A group photo of you with family or friends near one of your quilts on display

You might consider different photo caption styles, such as:
- Name of piece, year made, size of piece, materials used, owner of the piece
- Paragraph describing your inspiration for making the piece

Be sure to give the photographer credit for his or her images in your catalog. If there is one photographer, you might place this credit on the copyright page or in your essay. If there are multiple photographers, you might list the name of the photographer with each photograph.

If you have photographs of anyone other than yourself in your catalog, be sure to get a signed photo release from each person in the photo. Be sure you have their written permission to publish their image. You can go to a search engine and type "photo release form" for sample forms.

You'll need digital images to insert into your Word file. For CreateSpace, the final interior book file size cannot be larger than 400MB.

Just like with typing the manuscript exactly as it should be printed, your images should be 300 dpi and the exact size that you'd like them to appear in your catalog, *before* you put them into your manuscript. Save your images as TIFF files, not jpegs, for maximum print quality. ***Insert*** your photographs into your Word document; do not copy and paste the images, for best quality.

I am not a graphic designer, nor am I an expert on digital images. For technical questions, be sure to ask your print-on-demand company for their advice. CreateSpace has a free community discussion board that you can use.

Step 11: Type Your Artist Resume, Proof Manuscript

Your catalog is a great way for potential collectors of your work to become familiar with you. For people who have already invested in your work, this catalog may enhance the value of your quilts. The artist resume is a way to illustrate your involvement with your craft in a more formal way than the essay you've written for the catalog. The table below lists areas you might want to include.

Feature	Your Artist Resume Notes
How to Contact You	Website URL:
	Email address:
Exhibits or Shows	
Books or Articles	
Collectors	
Grants/Fellowships	
Workshops or Lectures	
Guild Memberships	
Education	

Quilt guilds, which create a catalog for a guild exhibit, may consider offering a page with the guild's history. Readers of the catalog may want to know when the guild was founded, who the founding members were, what major programs the guild sponsors, and how to get in touch or join the guild.

Galleries may consider listing the featured artist's resume, a biographic page about the gallery, or a listing of the guild's calendar of exhibits.

WOW! Once you've typed your artist resume, you're nearly done. Again, proof your quilt catalog manuscript. Ensure any purposely blank pages are indeed blank. Check for grammatical errors, readability, formatting consistency and such. For a week or two put your manuscript aside; then, come back to it with fresh eyes. Proof your manuscript again. You'll need an error-free file to create your quilt or art catalog.

Step 12: Open POD Account, Set up Book, Get ISBN

For this project consider using CreateSpace to publish your quilt or art catalog. CreateSpace is an Amazon owned company. CreateSpace printed books can also be purchased on Amazon, where many potential catalog buyers have accounts. Your quilt catalog will automatically have the Look Inside!™ feature when your catalog is on Amazon. This feature allows potential buyers to preview pages of your catalog. With CreateSpace you can also choose to offer your catalog to outlets, such as other major online bookstores and libraries.

To publish your catalog, visit CreateSpace.com to **sign-up** for a free member account. Be sure to read the Member Agreement carefully as this is a contract.

Gather the information below to help you to set up your catalog project.

	Your Catalog Notes
Your Project Name	
Title ID from CreateSpace:	Record here:
Book Title	
Book Subtitle	
Author's Name	
Secondary Author	
Book Description	You'll need to write your quilt or art catalog description as you would like it to appear on your Amazon book detail page. Use no more than 4,000 characters. This description may also be used for your book's back cover text, if you'd like.
ISBN-13	CreateSpace offers ISBNs or you may use one you own. Record your ISBN here:
Interior Type	
Book Size	
Word file name	

Once you upload your Word file, you can see if there are potential problems with your file using the CreateSpace Interior Reviewer. Your document is presented in a virtual book format. It's a thrill to use this tool to see how your catalog may look! Potential formatting errors will be highlighted. You can correct these errors before your potential customers buy your catalog.

Step 13: Create Your Catalog Book Cover

Now that you have your book interior uploaded to CreateSpace, it is time to create your quilt or art catalog cover.

CreateSpace has a free Cover Creator tool with dozens of cover templates based on your book's trim size. At the appropriate time, select "Build Your Cover Online." You don't have to be a graphic designer or computer wizard to use this free tool. Look over the different cover templates for your book size and select one. Don't worry; if you later decide to change your mind and want a new template, you can easily change templates before finalizing your project. I used the Cover Creator to design this workbook cover! When your book is printed, CreateSpace will apply your ISBN and bar code automatically.

Some of the information below may be needed to create your quilt catalog cover.

	Your Catalog Notes
Theme or Template used	
Title	
Subtitle	
Author(s)	
Front cover image	
Back cover image	
Back cover text	
Imprint name/logo, if you have one	
Background color	
Front color	

Once you are pleased with your cover design, select "Cover Complete."

Now that both your interior and cover are loaded, submit your files for review. It may take up to 48 hours for your files to be reviewed by CreateSpace.

Once your files have been approved by CreateSpace, order a proof of your quilt catalog. **Do not skip this step.** Order your proof to ensure that there are no errors in printing of your catalog. If something is wrong, fix the error(s), upload your corrected file(s), and repeat the process until you have a proof you approve.

Let me tell you – there is nothing like the moment you open the package from the mail with your proof. You fold back the packing materials and see YOUR quilt catalog with YOUR name on it. WOW!

Step 14: Select Your Channels, Direct Deposit Method, Book Description

While you are waiting to hear if your catalog cover and interior files have been approved, you can go to the **Distribute tab** and select the channels for your quilt or art catalog to be available through. Your free membership on CreateSpace includes automatic distribution of your quilt catalog on Amazon. Once you give final approval for your catalog to be sold, you'll see your catalog's detail page on Amazon within 5 to 7 business days.

From personal experience, I know how exciting it is to see a book appear on Amazon! Your quilt catalog's detail page is likely to build over a couple days. First the title and author's name may appear on Amazon.com. Then your book description will appear. It may take another day for your book cover to show up on the page.

You can also pay a modest fee (which at the time of this writing is $25) to participate in the CreateSpace Expanded Distribution program, which exposes your quilt catalog to bookstores and other online distribution points. If you used a CreateSpace ISBN, your quilt catalog may also be ordered by libraries and other academic institutions.

You are now ready to provide your **Royalty Payment information**. You'll need to let CreateSpace know, through its secure website, where to deposit your catalog royalties. The information you need to provide includes: your tax payer ID, your bank name, checking or savings account number, and bank routing number. The site will report your royalties to the IRS for tax purposes.

CreateSpace does provide instructions for non-US citizens to complete the tax information.

The **Description** section outlines additional information needed to promote and categorize your book. Two areas you might want to research first are the BISAC category and search keywords for your quilt or art catalog. BISAC stands for Book Industry Standards and Communications. The BISAC categories aggregate books by subject matter. You'll need to select the appropriate code for your catalog. Examples may include:

- Art/Individual Artist
- Biography & Autobiography/Artist, Architect, Photographer
- Crafts & Hobbies/Quilts and Quilting
- Crafts & Hobbies/Mixed Media

You'll also need to select up to five search keywords or phrases that potential readers would use to find your book. The keywords you brainstormed on in Step 6 to develop your catalog's title and subtitle will be helpful here.

Step 15: Set Your Retail Price

PUBLISHING IS A BALANCING ACT! VISIT PUBLISHYOURQUILTS.BLOGSPOT.COM

I've seen some self-published, full-color art catalogs with high page counts and equally high retail prices. For unknown quilt and textile artists, a high catalog price is sure to limit sales potential. You'll need to balance your catalog's price and sales potential.

CreateSpace has a tool you can use to determine your catalog's retail or list price based on the book's trim size, whether the interior is full-color or not, and how many pages are in your catalog. The amount of royalties paid to you is based, in part, by the list price you set for your catalog. Use the table below to record your potential royalty based on the CreateSpace Royalty Calculator.

Book size _____ Page count _____

If List Price is ...	Royalty from one book sold on Amazon	Royalty from a book sold via Expanded Dist.	Your Notes
$			
$			
$			
$			

Step 16: Celebrate the Publication of Your Catalog

Now that you have your published quilt or art catalog, it is time to celebrate and tell others about your work. Let PublishYourQuilts.blogspot.com know when your book is available to purchase. Email me at Black.Threads@yahoo.com. I'm happy to blog about your new catalog!

Make a list of the others you want to let know about your quilt or art catalog.

	Your Notes:
Family	
Neighbors/Friends	
Co-workers	
Quilt Guild(s)	
Association(s)	
Quilt magazine(s)	
Bloggers	

Social Media:
  Facebook
  LinkedIn
  Goodreads
  Pinterest	

Step 17:   Use Amazon to Market Your Quilt Catalog

Once your fabulous catalog is live on Amazon, take a moment to set up a free **Author Central** account at authorcentral.amazon.com. Author Central allows you to create a profile about you as an author and "tie" your new catalog to your profile. As you publish more books, they can also be "tied" to your profile. When someone searches your name on the site, your book title *and* your author profile will come back in the search results. An added benefit of an Author Central account is that Amazon will share retail sales figures for your quilt catalog by week and by US city and state – for free! Take a moment to visit the site to learn more.

When your catalog is published, you'll also want to "tag" it. Tags are keywords or categories that one can associate with your book. Tags help group similar books. So, if someone is looking for books about "religious quilts," books with "religious" and "quilts" in the title as well as books tagged "religious quilts" are likely to show in Amazon search results. Tagging your quilt catalog will expose more potential customers to your book. On your book's Amazon page, scroll down until you see the section that says "**Tags Customers Associate with This Product**." You can personally add up to 15 tags per book once your catalog is live on the site.

Assignments:

1. Create your author profile using Author Central.
2. Brainstorm potential tags for your book.
3. Visit competitive book titles on Amazon and note the tags you might also want for your quilt or art catalog in the table below.
4. Apply tags to your quilt catalog page on Amazon.

Book #1	Book #2	Book #3	Your Catalog Tags

Step 18: Keep Track of Your Expenses and Revenue

The focus on this series of blog posts was to illustrate how you can successfully publish your own quilt catalog using print-on-demand. You can go the DIY route with minimal expense, or you can outsource different aspects of the publishing process. You can keep track of potential expenses in the table below:

	Amount	Notes
Manuscript writing		
Photographs		
ISBN		
Editing/Proofreading		
Book Formatting		
Cover Design		
Distribution		
Proof Copy		
Copies you order		

Book sales are likely to come from two sources: personal sales and CreateSpace. You can keep track of your sales in the table below:

Month	Units Sold	Revenue	Notes

Make Notes for Your Next Quilt Catalog

I hope you enjoyed the PublishYourQuilts blog posts and workbook. Take a few moments to record what you've learned about your experience self-publishing your own quilt or art catalog. Are there things you would do differently next time?

Certainly you have ideas for another catalog. Feel free to use the space below to brainstorm new catalog ideas.

About the Author

Kyra E. Hicks is a quilter. Her quilts have appeared in more than forty exhibits in the United States and abroad. Her *Black Barbie Quilt* is in the permanent collection of the Fenimore Art Museum in Cooperstown, New York, as is her *Patriotic Quilt* at the Museum of Arts & Design in New York City.

Kyra loves historical, investigative research and rediscovering the lives of quilters past. She lives in Arlington, Virginia, where she tends her colorful, fragrant rose garden.

If you have enjoyed this workbook, you might enjoy other books by Kyra:

- *Black Threads: An African American Quilting Sourcebook*
- *Martha Ann's Quilt for Queen Victoria*
- *This I Accomplish: Harriet Powers' Bible Quilt and Other Pieces*
- *The Lord's Supper Pattern Book: Imagining Harriet Powers' Lost Bible Story Quilt*
- *1.6 Million African American Quilters: Survey, Sites, and a Half-Dozen Art Quilt Blocks*
- *Liberia: A Visit Through Books* – primary author, Izetta Roberts Cooper
- *The Return of the Guinea Fowl: An Autobiographical Novel of a Liberian Doctor* – primary author, Henry Nehemiah Cooper, M.D.

Made in the USA
Charleston, SC
17 March 2012